Sudden White Fan

Sudden White Fan

Poems by Veronica Patterson

Cherry Grove

Published by Cherry Grove Collections
P.O. Box 541106
Cincinnati, OH 45254-1106

ISBN: 978-1-62549-260-9

Poetry Editor: Kevin Walzer
Business Editor: Lori Jareo

Visit us on the web at www.cherry-grove.com

Cover design: Gary Steiner

For Evan Rice, Carrie Lee, Sara McLean
and Megan Colwell, the apples of my eye,
the orchard of my being.

Table of Contents

Acknowledgments

"Albedo," *GSU Review* (now *New South*)

"Cloudy," *Dogwood: A Journal of Poetry and Prose*

"Driving Back from the Wellness Clinic," published as "The
Etymology of Intersect," *Spoon River Poetry Review*

"Finches,"*Southern Poetry Review*

"Hair," *IMPROV*

"Like This," *Matter*

"Migration," *Poetry on Track* (anthology)

"The No Poem," *Malahat Review*

"The Other Wing," *Marginalia*. Revised.

"Perseids, Later," *Driftwood Review*

"Small Geometries," *Pinyon Review*

"Song of the Rising Amazement," *10x3*

"Soul, You Quaint Proposition," *10x3*

"Stephen's Tulips," *Spillway*

"To You, Pain," Honorable Mention, Tor House Competition,
2012, selected by Cornelius Eady. Website and
newsletter publication.

"Unfolding," *Pilgrimage*

"A Wave Crossing the Ocean," *New Millennium*

"What Is Given," published as "New Zealand," *Spillway*

Like This?

"The deep world is as clear as the surface one,
only it asks more of us."

Ortega y Gasset, *Meditations on Quixote*

On the bedroom window
the sun descending
lights evidence
of a bird
flown into it, dust

print of the whole,
both wings wide
as arms surrendering
the smudge of body.

What fills
the delicate fan of feathers
with such grief?
Some record

of the bird's surprise:

the *stop* of it–
so much like
shock
at how the world acts –

is –
some days
glass-flat and
unforgiving

yet the dust traces *like this—*

I. Sand Hill Cranes Migrating

To Tell a Story

You start to tell a story.

It's about your daughter or your begonia

or your cat. How it died or you thought it might die

or it didn't die but you know it will

and knowing weighs you down

but lifts it up, the cat or the begonia,

which is beginning to bloom, or the daughter,

who is also, into a light so bright you can't see

and your tongue dries

and all the words trail off

into radiance.

Then your neighbor walks in. He thinks

it's his geranium you're speaking of,

the green spice on his fingers

from breaking off even a dead leaf

and the hairs of his dog—

but you insist it's your cat you're talking about—

stick to the fingers and smell like begonias

or like your daughter just come in

from cutting lilacs in the yard, and you despair
over begonias, geraniums, all the blooming
daughters.

Then you recall a gardenia
browning at the edges
of your first dance and suddenly you think
life is like that, browning at the edges
before you realize
you talk begonia
and he listens geranium
and you're both wrong, but quiet
in a silence browning at the edges
when you start
to tell a story.

Perseids

I convinced my two daughters
to come out and watch
for meteors because

growing up, I lay in sultry
August dark, looking
for some swift light, some promise

to punctuate the days. On the porch
we leaned back in chairs,
singing half or less of old songs,

crooning into the blue-black
that licked our citronella candle's
lozenge of light. Sometimes

we only knew the chorus. Feet
on the stone railing,
tipped almost past balance,

the year, everything ripe

to shift. How could we know

when? Not that the moment

stood for anything exactly

— separate, particular —

but that it stayed with me

when the rest of the year—

all the *events*—

faded.

Driving Back from the Wellness Clinic Before Dawn

—inter- + secare *to cut, more at* SAW—

Intersection, a truck just misses us—the driver
never sees

I see the narrow gap,
disturbed spring air.

At home I take supplements
for heart, bones,

memory. And enter the next
hour. The next hour, slowly

wedging open. The next hour,
which opens! The sun

comes up. The day remains
supple. What had I been

saying? Was it I love you?
How easily nothing

happens. A tiny draft
from a slit

in space and time,
a sudden curiosity

about the shared root
of *oblivious* and *oblivion*.

The Clicking Beetles

Did my mother ever forgive my father
for falling off the rim of the Grand Canyon as we camped
from New York to California? Our tent was barely illumined
that morning by a few rays of sun rising. Only when I run
the film of memory in slow motion do I see
the exaggeration

of his pantomime—the stumble,
the shout, the arms wildly akimbo, then silence. The ledge
he had jumped to was four feet down. But now I recall
how many pranks they played on each other. Though this
one terrified me, it may have taken only coffee and a few
brilliant stratified vistas

for it to evaporate between them
or perhaps the glory of double rainbows above the stump
where my youngest brother, five, sat eating breakfast
from a tin plate, looking anointed in misty light. We all
recall it, and my sister with her Brownie camera
snapped a photograph.

Beyond was the vast

canyon, shadows without foreshadowing—her drinking, his

silence. True, she never left him, except for wild night drives.

Nor did he leave her. As soon as possible, we sisters

and one brother spun off elsewhere. Last to leave

was the one who had looked up

       at the shutter's click,

who lived longest inside the damaging story. Who

fell and fell. Is broken. Who got lost despite

those promising rainbows. At the canyon that day

the sun finished rising and the startling beetles

began again to click and leap.

Cloudy

A poem makes choices—for example, to speak of clouds or
death. The poem prefers clouds. The poet prefers clouds, the
way they suggest palaces and full sails. Then clouds let a
climbing light descend, Jacob's Ladder, thoughts of

angels and wrestling. Clouds throw a shadow in front of a
woman walking west, where vapor twines around mountain
peaks like hair caught in a brush. And she recalls rose-gold
clouds in leaving-light.. But it was morning when death

arrived—an infant—named, not yet known. There was, as is
said of some disasters, not-a-cloud-in-the-sky, though even a
poem knows better than to assume anything about loss or
weather. No cloud in the sky limited by her window,

just the hospital's shocking brick corner. *Something* shocking.
Lying still, she knows clouds are unruly, yet death had
towered fast and secretly, cloud by cloud, as an infant's stuffed
lamb lying wide-eyed on a small sheet

in a small room
    beneath a mobile
        of clouds slowly
            turning.

How to Section a Grapefruit

On this widening morning, it is
   yellow, round, radiant.
      I orbit

then slice the grapefruit, whose smell engulfs me, as I
   arrive at the core of ripeness,
      tart and sweet, its edge

acidic:
   a garden with a wall where one can't stay. Two
      either.

I am preparing it
   for us. Traced, could I know
      how any of us came exactly here?

If its workers were migrant, immigrant?
   If it had been
      picked with bitterness?

When I first saw a grapefruit knife and spoon,
    I knew the world was full
        of special tools. Wanting

to get things right, I would ask and ask
    what is that? Yet I've told you nothing
        precise about this grapefruit. And nothing

about my love. Serrated words
    circle, section, don't remove
        the zest.

Its design is one of sections,
    stanzas, to hold the juice.
        The grapefruit

cannot be approached,
    only eaten.

Distillation, Was This?

—for my chemist father, at the last

Did he forget—or did the fever urge him
to summon, then dismiss—the first image
of her, who was not so much chosen as already
in him, as she came down the brick
steps of her parents' house?

Did he forget, or inside delirium remember
the steering wheel in the car orbiting the race course
at Watkins Glen, his hands, world simplified
to strategy, edge, slip-stream. Or was each turn
a whirl in their first dance?

And how easily could he forget the children,
or remember the happy tumult of their births
yet lose the complicated landscape,
the fields through which the good dogs
leaped and barked with glee.

Once he went to France, the summer away

from the misery of home—of the pump struck by lightning,

car breaking down, rented house too far outside town.

At the Eiffel Tower, which he must have visited

between conference sessions, did he reach for her then,

the once-girl dissolving in liquid rituals.

Yet the image of that dress insistently white

as the sheets his body soaked—

and the one they would pull over all of him,

And was she there? Above him was a light

Or the largest mother-of-pearl button made

in the family's New York factory

traded for the yo-yo that won the contest

walk the dog around the world skin the cat loop-the-loop

held at the movie theater before the reel turned

and the story began.

Migration

how this day we had chilled
with narrow words
lifts by degrees and widens

when you bring home a section
of the newspaper folded to a photo—
two sandhill cranes, leaping,

intent on each other, and we are
once again standing on wheat stubble,
near wetlands, inside the ancient

cries of 10,000 migrating birds
with six-foot wingspans
spiraling up from a snow-streaked

field near Monte Vista—how close
we stood then—

Homing

They circle the way I circle a poem, three times around a clearing, a wide sweep to listen for the poem's own sound waves, not just mine. Then, when the loft is sure in mind, place they return to, they set off. But they are not geological surveyors, not lookouts, not angels, of course not, guardian or otherwise, so they can miss the way. The infrasound waves for navigation may be too low in frequency, less than 0.1 Hertz, though one home bears the name and pull of Ithaca. But I have two homes. Have I moved too far to this one, stayed longer than the allotted odyssey? Does one topography overlay and absorb the other? Or do they cancel and erase? Is there more to ask? Ignoring disturbances in field and atmosphere, steadied by some late-breaking release, I home—wings white in sun.

II. Soft _Who_ of Mourning Doves

My Summer Dream Job

was wet-copying student records at the university. There were
thousands, the chemicals heady in the old auditorium, where
my Arvin transistor radio played music. I sang and sang
—"Stranger on the Shore," "Moon River," "Where Have All
the Flowers Gone," "You Don't Know Me." I laid each copy to
dry on the steps and seats row by row, and re-gathered them
in sequence. For long stretches, I saw no one. By late
afternoon, melancholy came step by step down stairs toward
the stage and podium, but evaporated by morning. Outside,
ivy inched up the walls of buildings around the quadrangle. In
the basement, I ate my spare lunch among casts of Greek and
Roman sculptures cool to my touch. Was everything becoming
—I, meteor, spectrometer, northern lights, mossy rock,
cascading water? Before dusk, chimes sounded from the clock
tower. What dream wasn't alive in the echoing emptiness? At
home, my skin hummed all night. They were my first harvest,
those slightly rippled pages, each with an implied story—

brilliance, failure, sorrow, mediocrity, with only the alphabet keeping order.

To You, Pain

"...the darkness and the light
are both alike *to thee*..."

Psalm 139

You were there, a secret
when my flesh was knitted
in the womb, mistaking
over for under, left for right,

tangling strands of cells
you could not ravel, biding
your time. You were there
when a scalpel made

your works manifest,
watching from under
the numbness, waiting
to emerge. At night,

in the open, you stretched
each hour, leech
and atheist, breaking in
at 3 a.m., as if the incision

were a door left ajar.
When morphine came
you left, muttering,
but didn't go far. Let

go, let me go. You
were a lesson
I didn't want to learn,
my eraser,

smudging. You woke
more than the body—
you abraded *being*
until it knew itself.

After Long Illness, Instruction

From the window,
I watch a house finch, redbud of energy,
fly to an abandoned nest
in clematis on the porch

and nestle in tightly, inching down,
then shoot out, launched.

~~~

On a rare drizzly day,
mist above the lake's surface,
violet-green swallows
dip and rise, crisscrossing the lake.

After insects, yes—
but they loop an airy net.

~~~

I hear it first near dawn, the soft *who*
of mourning doves,
not so much question as
morning's record of the night.

Small heads, slender necks, Quaker selves—
teach me the slow lightening
of grief, the sudden white fan of ascent.

For Your Surgery, Vigilance

"Contemplate the elegance of infinity.
Don't ask 'When will I use this?'"
                                    Manil Suri

From my antique Tibetan singing
bowl resonance ripples out

and in, like the radiant energy of
some poems. I'm drawn to

the idea that all sounds emitted
are still out there somewhere,

ready to come to
the place I think of

and surround you—

an operating room where
on sterile sheets, your flesh

opens to air, light, blades. How
firmly I believe in your being

here without end. I contemplate
infinity's elegance now. I use it

sparingly, invoking its curved
ongoing glide.

Soul, You Quaint Proposition

—for K.J.

You milkweed pod
You nape of the day
You bucket in the rain
You half-hitch, you heave-ho
You editor of the heart
hairline crack
baroque protocol
nudge

You rototiller, circus roustabout,
elephant keeper, prod, grin
You rent flesh

You grand master of loss
You silence
You raised eyebrow
You itch, you insomniac
You janitor

You understudy for goddess

tattered joker

gargoyle

talk, talk, talking about *home*, no address

You with me

second navel

Midsummer Hour

"Among the … devastations of life is this then—
our friends are not able to finish their stories."

Virginia Woolf

You live on a small sweep of prairie.
Some of the grass burned, leaving
a black scorch. The first new blades
are not unlike the last strands
of your hair.
                  Despite the deliberate
inner holocaust, it is the tumors
that burgeon. The new drug regimen you begin
is just the new regimen. For my visit
I bring you books, one just published,
set safely in ancient times. In it
a strong woman defies the odds
of her world. The other, a beauty
of a story, which means in this case, alive

with love and war and loss. You are
matter-of-fact about how long
you can focus.

        I hate facts,
strict little terrorists hiding in cells. I wish
for you—tall willows, green-ash leaf shade,
relief from this constant noon
too much like dark.

Stephen's Tulips

—for Stephen Beal and his book of poems
about life and embroidery threads: *The Very Stuff*

Stephen gave me six tulip bulbs
from Amsterdam. I planted them
too deep to come up
every year. But this spring, Stephen

gone for six, I look out
the south window and catch my breath.
All six shot slender stems taller
than the other tulips, whose reds, yellows,

and stripes seem garish in comparison.
In a circle, they sway as if part of
an ancient ritual, a color I can't name,
but something required this vestal

coral—a cloud streaked with last light?—a hue

between the moment I call you to the window

and the moment you arrive. I take his book

with tabs of thread colors for each poem

to the garden and cup a cup of petals

in my hand. The outside of each petal

is matte, lighter than its shiny inside. I

match each to hues on a page. "Sisters,"

he called these shades. I buried the bulbs

beneath din and damage, where they pondered dirt—

that very stuff—then thrust green needles

into the fabric of light, then ascended.

The Red Chair

red chair, half in light

abraded into singing, did you say?

on stairs just around the corner

in Andre Kertesz's silver gelatin print
Chez Mondrian, Paris

red chair, in half light

I open my mouth and out falls
a passage of Goethe's *Faust*

was die Welt im Innersten
zusammenhält

magnetic north shifting

in the red folding chair

blue ischemic moon
thin ligature of clouds

what to play on reflected piano keys

awake to pain, saying words for

each yellow rectangle in the children's hospital opposite

the red chair

of Scriabin's 24 preludes, 13 through 19

red metal chair

before black threads caught on
his septicemia

and pain on a scale of one to
flames

morphine's little circus
animals, glitter around the room

red chair angled to the sill

through four window panes
tawny land, distant water

the metal dark within
green walls in which

why the ones who seared me with beauty

opened one door, red chair
in a bare room

near the corner

of the philosophical study of
the existence and the nature of being

I, hungry, fed, insatiable

in the red chair

unfolding

Sea Greens:

Thicketed edge of a lake where branches cascade to the surface. A canoe slides by, troubling the succulence.

Cusp of blue-green

The moment between 4 o'clock and longing. Glimmering. Tinted glass telephone insulation cap on the windowsill.

Bone turquoise

Dragonfly that became Queen of the Willows. The water in New Zealand, due to the Tyndall Effect.

Aquamarine

Effect of longer wavelength light transmitted, effect of particles, effect of your eyes. The first time I looked into them.

Paraiba tourmaline

Blue's question: "That night on the ocean island when the owl's wing brushed your hair—what green since?"

teal undercurrent

Ache of water parted by swans in Galway Bay. Sun on a vine hanging from a balcony in a city I haven't been to.

Remedy

—to the 90-year-old honey-locust tree

In October, after I fell and broke bones, you taught me
beauty by pain. Not *through*; I wasn't through. Yet every
branch offered a series of gold pinnate leaves, small oval
tickets to

what might be. You taught me November's imperative,
the *no-matter-what* of harvest, your seeds inside a twist
of helix. Pods hung until a hard wind threw their polished
mahogany across the yard

before sunset. But even at night in December, I saw
how your angled bare branches fractured the sky. You
stayed up with me. Moving slowly, I could hang
and rehang the full moon. Now

it's January, a new year. I know that the root of *heal* is *whole*.

The bones have done their part. And the root of *endure*

is *hard*. I close the dictionary, read through

the page of glass.

You Enter the Dream

You enter the dream like a room you don't remember renting, yet you have lived there always. Outside the window, a full moon rises.

You enter the dream of a round stone table, fruit and wine and bread, a place saved for you. They look up in greeting. The sun sets on vineyards that slope away in concentric circles.

You enter the dream in which a bird lands on your left shoulder to whisper words you can almost hear. In the morning, waking from sleep, you find a father. No—a feather.

You enter the dream in which the lost infant dances between her grandmother and great-grandmother, holding their hands. Dance of the spirits. Your hand stirs. Your mother stirs. Your mothering.

Even from the dream in which you are cut off from those close to you, first by fire, then water, you wake sweating, breathless, but new. Someone still beside you. The bird returns to your left shoulder, murmuring what hasn't happened.

You enter the dream like a room you don't remember renting, yet you have lived there always.
Outside the window, a full moon sets.

III. Section with No Birds

Despair Shovels the Driveway

"I advise you to despair."
—Søren Kierkegaard

Already Despair

wants the next storm

for its private

blank, for the way snow suggests action

& nothing.

Inside, Despair

smoothes sheets, lingering,

longs for later, recalls

the Chinese symbol

for *direction*, leaning.

At night Despair

trains the scope

on a moon

rough as pumice, all the while

thinking scrape & heave yet why

peel the new white

cover from

this hour? Heavy

swing

of the old shovel,

its dark metal

curled back

from both sides of the blade

as if it wanted to be beautiful

to snow. Only early

in a story is Despair virtuous.

Despair Does the Laundry

"The despairer understands that it is a weakness
to take the earthly so much to heart..."
—Søren Kierkegaard

Despair wants nothing left
in the clothes hamper &
water fills the drum,
lets go
of everything
intimate &
how centrifugal
the spin, *to flee from the center*
from stain's persistent geography &
the dryer lulling as enamel
the softener outdoor fresh &
towels blue as the frayed sky
how the one sock &
how flexible the hose &
how best not to think

of that

Despair can't choose

between a) press care,

b) wrinkle release,

c) air fluff,

or d) chime

how soft the lint,

how useless

Despair and the Dark

"Is there no manager? To whom
shall I make my complaint?"
—Søren Kierkegaard

Despair wonders how to
manage the dark. Cut a hole
and install a door-flap? This dark
already comes and goes on
its own. Fill a jar with fireflies,
punch a lid full of holes
with an ice pick? Childhood
is not enough. Weed it? This dark
isn't bindweed, though quick
to blossom,
vigorous, doubled
by frantic pulling. It's no companion,
though someone might think so
seeing Despair and the dark
at 3:00 a.m., elbows

on the kitchen table,

staring.

Despair Sets the Clocks Forward, Wondering

"But despair is held open every instant..."
—Søren Kierkegaard

there's

not enough dark

to hold

    Despair

hates spring,

       season, noun, & verb

the spiraling into

pollen, seeds,

trouble

the only true coils:

rattlesnake,

mortal,

rope

       how soon its leaps turn

       to shuffle &

       slough

or slough (the other pronunciation)

of despond,

Despair's

little joke

Despair Watches the Full Moon Set

"Take away paradox... and you have..."
—Søren Kierkegaard

it's not

the periodic return

of this disk of winter, not

the beauty, or not exactly,

not the clear gaze,

nor how the earth holds

its breath.

not the brilliant ice-path

over the lake, the slip

behind the bony ridge,

the final tease

of light, not the rush of grief

unmooring— first, Despair

craves

fullness, then

the sweet all

of gone

Despair at the Optometrist's

"I see it all perfectly;
there are two possible situations—"
—Søren Kierkegaard

At the optometrist's, Despair

can never say

which lens is clearer, one or

two, two or three, this

or that.

Despair & the Record-Breaking Pumpkin

"I rejoice for my joy, by, in, with, about, over, for and with...
a heavenly refrain which... interrupts our other singing..."
—Søren Kierkegaard

Despair stayed
up all night watching
the ropey vine
snake into the world
explode into bloom, feed
the green fist
that drank 200 gallons
of water a day &
grew 35 pounds each night
until, first jaundiced, then orange
it weighed more than a ton,
having sucked in world, every
mineral, star and story
and dreamed it
into a song of sorts

its voice deepening until

round as an opera singer

it sliced open a mouth

with a wicked, snaggle-toothed grin—

(seeds slid everywhere)

& trilled

into the local night

none shall sleep

Despair in the Womb &

"For to despair about the eternal is impossible
without having a conception of the self,
that there is something eternal in it..."
—Søren Kierkegaard

At first, only an inkling, thin
as a hair caught
in the mouth. Chafe
of a bent eyelash. Despair grew
cracks in everything,
though the floor held
and walls fell only in
dreams.
      The best Despair
could do was map the cracks
with a pen. *Hope* is Despair's second
syllable. And joy. Again.
      Prokofieff's *wrong note*
became the one cloud

on the music's horizon, then

the place the notes

returned to. Horse hair

in clay, burned away

in a kiln, became — becomes —

uncanny beauty, a bowl

of mane whipping in wind. Despair

sings *thou art* —

IV. What They Were Saying in Finch

The No Poem

—to S

The trouble with discipline
is the state of the world,
which makes me wonder

if that *no*, the one I would
reason you out of,
is the one syllable you'll need,

though this time
you use it wildly
against one teacher's unfair judgment
of someone else, and I, collaborator,
wish you'd be diplomatic, get along,
though I know where
we've gotten along to.

You hear me wonder
if that fierce sound
is mother to the future,

answer to something

we once thought unthinkable

but will think of

and you get away with it again.

Keep it away. Smuggle it deep

into another country

keep it alive

for the refusal

in which affirmation begins

like green come from red

blades plunging through earth

headlong and stubborn, before spring

with its sun and *yes*.

Albedo

~ Dusk. From the window
of what you call your life
you look into the yard.

~ On the lake, a line of Canada geese
glides by, each with an inch of snow
on its back.

~ By the blue spruce, a fox bounds
straight up, all four paws in air,
then buries its head
deep, flings snow over its back.

~ But what about the severing
world, child crying on a beach, hand
that was only choosing an orange
at the open market?

~ As the flakes drift down
light increases. Dark
forgets itself.

~ You feel— You want—
You want your words to—

~ Exuberance, flare,
mercy. How does snow
do that?

Hair

—a ghazal for E

I was instantly conscious of wind, how it pushed
from your forehead fine brown hair.
I blew into your face from the direction of your journey, lifting
your hair.

I kept you spellbound with my story, folded it into a fan, then
a bird,
which landed as if to nest, coaxing your credulous fingers into
my hair.

We tangled our lives, but you had to leave. When you
returned, you saw how long I
had grown the hair you touched—enough for two daughters
with barrettes in their hair

(and the black-haired daughter, who unfastened). But the
sisters used soft brushes
with yellow handles, curl and uncurl, until the bristles grew
sturdy, long enough

to French braid for departure. When they visit, they leave long
floating strands I wind
around my finger as if I could hold them safe by keeping their
hair.

We know: One day clouds will shadow air that closes where
we were and blow away.
And, yes, ash will secretly mingle what must have flamed first
—this perilous hair.

But at last I can speak of my tortoiseshell comb, with our
shared V on its rib,
which groomed your fate to the same angle as mine—did it
seem chance?—it was hair.

Daughter, Apostrophe

—to C

At night, holding flashlights, we train
cans of spray paint to a fine stream,

begin with local signs, My Papas Place,
The Cats Meow, amend the bank's "next days"

to "next day's" to make our small deposits
available sooner. Then we take a road trip,

city after city, like Edward Abbey's
Monkey Wrench Gang, but with

a different cause: punctuation.
We use *The Chicago Manual of Style,*

thick, inexorable. Even young, you took
to the dense ones, the sweep of Shakespeare,

Dickens, Woolf, and said, "more." Then

became an actor, each role studied

and absorbed to become repeatable

fire. Keats wrote "O, brightest..." I sing

you— in this, my apostrophe:

possessed, you illuminate the wild

precise syntax of the world

in its mirror.

Small Geometries

1. Alignment

From voices around the table,
chaotic ideas emerge, quicken,
and shape-shift.

Your slow fingers
reach for my quick ones,
sidling up, like a whisperer
nearing a skittish horse.

Talk moves too fast
to be gathered, sorted,
arranged.

But placemat and napkin, knife,
fork and spoon, those
I can align and realign
again and again.

2. Angle & Arc

At the kitchen table, the evenings
of oblong days, we sit right-angled,
turned to each other, a candle burning
midway down our hypotenuse.

Once, I stayed in a round house
alone, wished for a crescent bed
to echo the moon above the skylight.
But then I returned to you
through our rectangular door.

Thereafter, I angled chairs
across corners; only your
long couch hugs the wall—
but I skew the chairs across from it.

In restaurants, the two of us
in a curved booth
slide around the arc until
we can see each others' faces.

3. Dimensions

A tick and the distant whoosh
of tiny flames as the boiler comes alive
a floor below, then water ripples down
the walls of this aquarium. Outside
the moon glitters on the lake, and light shifts
and eddies on the bedroom walls.
If the middle shade is raised and a car drives down

the street to the far lake shore, headlights flood

the headboard and wood grain flows. Then

I know *being*, how watery, and I drift

to the living room, where the paintings

have grown strange and luminescent.

I don't wake you because I don't know

if you have gills for this or I need

to swim alone.

A Wave Crossing the Ocean

"I believe in the refusal to take part."
        Wislawa Szymborska

I was crossing the ocean
trying to maintain equanimity,
avoiding the glitz of white-sand
beaches, pushing back hard, flailing,

but afraid of becoming a wrecking
surge, a tsunami. Still I gained debris,
not just islands of plastic, but the couch
where a grandfather had been napping,

a stove and refrigerator now rusting
into a marriage, a tricycle
with pink handlebars, the collar and tags
of a dog named Dickens, a cello, a single

oar, the most exotic orchid

from the flower shop in the square

where everyone came to buy gifts for

birthdays and anniversaries. Flotsam

without jetsam. I tried to discard

the bodies, let bones go, shrug

them off in deep swells, but whole

neighborhoods rumpled the surface

and only the smallest bodies drifted away

easily, those I would have

cradled in a trough

and rocked.

Unfolding

When you were six,
older boys on the school bus
ripped your valentine
and I, waiting at the stop
to walk you home, shook with rage,
mended it with tape.

I still want to give you
refuge—stand between you
and each available ruin
but you outfox me.

Remember how in school
we were given a diagram,
the outline of a building—
and had to imagine the structure
it folded into?

I've made a café

where you can sit

in a blue chair at a yellow table.

Through the door, a fingering breeze

from the ocean.

Over a cup of fragrant

black coffee, you open

a newspaper to job ads,

apartments for rent, pick up

a pen to circle a new life.

Finches

The clematis quivers
when they return

to the porch trellis.
The leaf blower blasted

their nest sideways
and emptied it. Now

they circle back, circle
back, voices wrenched.

A code for disaster?
One pulls out a single twig.

Are they saying in finch
oh my god, oh my god

as we do at the news
of hurricane, tumor, fire?

What Is Given

Your bones are long. My hands
are different sizes. Neither of us
gardens. Your father was *a good man*—
when they said that. Your mother
was a lily. My mother was an equation
my father couldn't solve. All of them
gone. Now
shall we go to New Zealand?

V. White Peacock Now

Itinerary

—Arrowtown, New Zealand

A round table of latticed metal, a stone-paved courtyard
  where we sat in sun scattered by the leaves
    of a tree we couldn't name.

We'd finished the walking tour, seen miners' cottages,
  St. Mary MacKillup's school for the poor.
    We came for the history.

It was February, winter at home, but here, late summer,
  mornings cool. Folded over every other chairback,
    a woven red shawl.

There must have been sounds. The chink of cups. The nearby
  grind of coffee, hiss of steam. Voices
    I didn't hear.

Time circled and came close, drifted away as we dropped

back to autumn in Michigan, coffee break,

from the graduate school

library. As we stirred small vortexes in our cups, talking,

no one could have known how far we'd gone.

How far we'd come.

News of the World, 1887

—after Van Gogh's *Grapes, Lemons, Pears, and Apples*

Nothing holds still. Lemons import a sharp light. The purple grapes have left behind the vineyards of history, which makes them luminous and sweet. The green grapes are like painters; even their jealousies have a certain flair. Yellow leaves gesture to autumn. Someone brought them in—rather than sorrow or ashes—from a walk. Here, they itch for wind and field again. One of five apples hurries off the canvas. Such *leaving*. But then, just for a moment, each fruit ponders its personal how-I-came-to-be-in-the-studio-this-morning. Hosting paint. None can imagine its long role as *the past*. Or see stems as wicks. The cosmos swirls here as a tablecloth, serving up everything. Note the rare pigment *burnt joy*.

They Said the Astonishing Blue

—inter-island flight, New Zealand

in the Queenstown water was due to
the Tyndall Effect. Recent flooding, minerals

bonded to water molecules, blue light waves
scattering intense and long. But I thought it was

because we had flown all night over ocean
to this country where people might have hung

upside down in grade-school diagrams
of the world. So when I lost you

at the airport, though for a short

eternity, I felt how thin the membrane

was over the nothing, the void

that goes all the way

down to a sad aquifer.

I murmured to myself,

everything will be all right, as people say,

all shall be well, as

Julian of Norwich said, but I didn't

believe a word of it, or only one: *all*. Nothing

here helped: the huge Moreton Bay fig tree

overwhelmed me. Here, birds had forgotten

how to fly, volcanoes barely slept beneath
sham vegetation. Tectonic plates collided.

Everyone said no I haven't seen him. So
when I finally saw you I was furious

with terror, cold in this borrowed
summer. In the first autumn of our regard

then love, the one we'd come here
to celebrate, the original

falling, I thought I fell
far. That was nothing.

The Other Wing

All over the world, people flap in awkward circles,

insisting— *I am not this wing. I'm the other.*

Some forget wings when they wake up,

but that's not safe. On the anniversary of my wing,

I sit on the kitchen counter with ripening fruit. I'm a wing

not flight. The ache of another wing coming, miserable ecstasy,

a kind of teething, tight hot skin, white pushing.

I pluck and set the table with only the feathers

my guests understand. After dinner, they leave

me slowly refeathering. The other wing,

drawn by my tenacity or glue, comes as I slump, says, *Get up.*

Though it's midnight, I make the other a sandwich,

remove the crust— *Thanks. I needed something*, it says.

How about some insomnia? I ask. The days go by; I cut them

into quarters. The other wing is lonely. I could ask it over

to talk about the big thief. But days pass like white plates

that should be red. Luckily, you can advance by mistake,

like the heroines in nineteenth-century novels. At last

I go to the other wing, ask, *Where's my pen?*

Don't laugh—I'm told to pluck and sharpen

a swan's primary flight feather. I say, *I wish this were all*

metaphor. It's been a long haul with barely a moment

for myself. The other wing finds me

tiring. This is how it always happens: One day

you peck away some shell. You like the soft half-light.

But the next day wind pushes in, cracks everything

open.

Song of the Rising Amazement

Is the rising amazement
moonlight falling on a terrace? On
a woman? A man at a door watching
the woman? The door?

The grass of heaven,
the heaven of grass
comes to them. They brace to live
in the radiance
of rising amazement. But what
is its radius, its circumference?

They solve for pi. Astonishing!

Not stopping
at 3.14159265, they sail

decimal waves — to

the feverish core of the earth,

into the unbound trunk

of the sky. Though they are not

mathematicians, the night receives

their counting and reverberates

splendor.

In the rising amazement,

moonlight falls on a terrace.

A man calls to a woman

in the doorway. The woman

turns to him.

Walk Up

—sheep station, New Zealand

Because I was on the other side of the earth
    it seemed right that the swans
        were black. We had seen

dolphins, steaming turquoise pools
    in volcanic valleys, glow worms hanging deep
        in pitch-dark caves, yet

what echoes in me:
    watching the sheep dog work
        scattered sheep

in silence. The dog's head
    just above grass,
        focused on them,

he, steadily moving,

    forward, a slight feint

        and the man murmuring

           walk up   walk up   walk up

and the sheep molded,

    then urged

        to the gate. I want that

deep attention in my days.

To the White Peacock of We Shall All Be Changed

Nothing
is like your impossible lace,
swinging open. Watchers
lift cameras between
retina and world, as if *being*
itself burned white-hot.

Not everything
without color
is albino. Like this page.
Feathers have thousands
of flat branches, each full
of bowl-shaped indentations,
tiny prisms that fan light into
iridescence.

One true thing

And just as

one learns how to adjust

the naked eye, everything

clothes itself. Closes.

Some things

first bitter on the tongue

are sweet after.

Lake Morning, Solstice

A Japanese watercolor—
    the lake still, one grebe gliding
        mountains twice, Longs,

Meeker, the Mummy Range, Indian
    Peaks. Cottonwood seeds speckle
        the surface, a dotted Swiss dream

of summer. Aside from our paddles
    dripping, this floating world is quiet.
        We pause to meditate, as the almost

level light of sun coming gently
    insists. The word *perfect* hovers
        and flits like a blue dragonfly. Our

voices murmur. Mine, of how the wall
    of the canyon catches the sun. Yours,
        of light on the Palisades.

We've said these things before, but some words
bear repeating. Even our canoe
is green.

Perseids, Later

A tease of clouds intermits
the searing blueblack. Cicadas
drone in a 3 a.m. silence
　　and I fall back

onto an Army blanket, 1956,
a meadow outside Ithaca, lying with sister
and brother, in the grip of fierce
　　dreams and longings, my skin

alive with *up,*
drawn to the studded dark, whose
tiny burns might be those of a sparkler
　　twirled too fast.

This night, as you sleep inside,
I lift binoculars to contain
these pricking lights, which
　　perforate,

and still pull me

to them. Your dream wafts from the house,

a stay. In waning heat, in my thin

   nightshirt, I feel

   the years accordion,

and I shiver. Each of us

gets to be vast sometime. Three

   meteors streak

   the length

of a star-glazed strand

of my hair. *How can the birds sleep*

   in this confetti of light.

how I tell it now

I have not said exactly enough how the woods, how the deep
shale gorges, the damp of mosses, their little worlds, green
cushioning. how the young fields of Queen Anne's lace and
later the bent goldenrod. how scarlet the sumac. how the old
apple orchard poured that insistent cider, even then. how the
snow falling. how violets hid. how I tell it now.

how the ache of a dissolving brother won't. how can I keep
from singeing? how black the edges. how to include
the raven, raucous ebony, pulsating. how the bitter is
made sweet. *how* refined, by what method? how I ask
and ask. how wonder intrudes. how the great blue heron
stalks through layers of existence. how I tell it now.

how Sisley painted and I read of him, then saw the snowy
alley! how he wasn't among the luminaries. how he caught
the tremulous everything. how *Flood at Port-Marley*,
disaster composed, yet redeems light and color. how
Renoir's *On the Terrace* seems mother and daughter, still.
how longing shapes looking. how I tell it now.

how I have forgotten the young fox, wisp of russet on asphalt my car did not hit. how I have forgotten too many teachers, but not Elizabeth, not Lisel, and not the one I can't. how inexactly forgotten the day in the gold woods, my lucky *no*. how I drove west to *yes*. how it's never quite, then unaccountably is. how sudden the white fan. how I tell it now.

Veronica Patterson is a Phi Beta Kappa graduate of Cornell University, the University of Michigan, the University of Northern Colorado, and the Warren Wilson College MFA program. Her poetry collections are *How to Make a Terrarium* (Cleveland State University, 1987); *Swan, What Shores?* (NYU Press Poetry Prize, 2000), which was a finalist for the Academy of American Poets' 2000 James Laughlin Award and won awards from both the Colorado Center for the Book (Colorado Book Award for Poetry) and Women Writing the West (Willa Award); *Thresh & Hold*, which won the Gell Poetry Prize (Big Pencil Press, 2009) and was a finalist for the 2010 Colorado Book Award for Poetry; and *& it had rained* (WordTech Communications, CW Books, 2013). She has also published two chapbooks *This Is the Strange Part* (Pudding House Publications, 2002, prose poems) and *Maneuvers: Battle of the Little Bighorn Poems* (Finishing Line Press, 2013), as well as a collection of poetry and photography, *The Bones Remember: A Dialogue*, with photographer Ronda Stone. Her poems have appeared in numerous publications including *The Southern Poetry Review, The Louisville Review, The Sun, The Madison Review, The Malahat Review, The Indiana Review, Another Chicago Magazine, The Mid-American Review, The Willow Review, The Montserrat Review, The Bloomsbury Review, Willow Springs, The Colorado Review, The Midwest Quarterly, Many Mountains Moving, Coal City Review, Dogwood, New Letters, The Bellingham Review, Cimarron Review, The Beloit Poetry Journal, Runes, Pilgrimage, Prairie Schooner, Lumina, Rosebud, Spoon River Poetry Review, Snake Nation Review,*

Driftwood Review, and *Pinyon Review.* Her poems "Around the Block of the World" and "The Samovar" co-won the 2006 Campbell Corner Poetry Prize. Patterson has been awarded artists' residencies at the Ucross Foundation, Rocky Mountain National Park, Hedgebrook, the Ragdale Foundation, and the Gell Center. She received two Individual Artist's Fellowships from the Colorado Council on the Arts. Poems have been nominated for a Pushcart Prize several times. Her essays have appeared in *The Georgia Review, PieceWork Magazine,* and *Pilgrimage.* Her essay "Comfort Me with Apples" was selected as a Notable Essay of the Year.

Made in the USA
Columbia, SC
09 July 2018